With love,

Aug 2019

THE BOOK OF LOVE

"O Lord, I ask for Your love, the love
of those who love You, and the love of
everything that brings me closer
to Your love"

PROPHET MUHAMMAD ﷺ
Authentic collection of Tirmidhi

THE BOOK OF LOVE

Muhammad ibn Yahya al-Ninowy

ISBN 978-0-9862664-3-0   paperback
ISBN 978-0-9862664-4-7   e-book

Library of Congress Control Number: 2017959410

Printed in Canada

Contents

INTRODUCTION

Love is a journey everyone should consciously and actively take. The journey is more amazing than our greatest aspirations and more miraculous than our most beautiful dreams. The journey leads the wayfarer to personal liberation, whose highlights are love, forgiveness, unconditional compassion, mercy, reconciliation, hope, happiness, positive contribution and optimism, with no place at all for repression, original sin, judgment, punishment, guilt, pain, enmity, or even death.

This is not just possible, this is real and beautiful. The journey on the path of love is the elixir of an everlasting life of love. There is no shortage of love, just our willingness to embrace it with our whole heart and channel it to others.

The Book of Love is a window into the journey of the wise throughout our human history, such as: Adam, Abel, Noah, Abraham, Joseph, Moses, Jesus and Muhammad. It is Islam, as I know it.

Though *The Book of Love* is a book of personal reflections, each line of its aphorisms is an opener to a more intimate inner conversation.

Welcome to the world of love.

Muhammad ibn Yahya al-Ninowy

The All-Loving sent His beloved
out of love, to teach love
with love to love for love.

Awakening to Self-Realization

1. Spiritual diseases affect your heart, which becomes blind with sins, and can only be healed by sincere repentance.

2. The one whose heart died by heedlessness
    of Him, will not be awakened by afflictions,
    generally.

3. The afflicted is not the one who is suffering from the pain of calamities, rather, it is the one whose heart is no longer connected to Allah[1] Ta'ala,[2] thereby losing vision, feeling, and self.

---

1 The Creator of all.
2 Exalted.

4. If you are absent in your prayers, your fasting is starvation and thirst, and your response to His continuous kindness to you is complaints, then you need a heart.

5. The true Muslim is the one who is in total *salām*.[3]
   Islam means *salām*. The key to *salām* is total
   submission to Him with the mind and heart, not
   just body and tongue.

---

3 Inner peace, tranquility, submission, and spiritual
   illumination.

6. When they wake up, the people of *ghafla*[4] check their *dunya*[5], the people of *dhikr*[6] check their *ākhira*,[7] and the people of Allah Ta'āla check their hearts with Him.

---

4 Absenteeism.
5 This world.
6 Remembering Him *Subhanāhu wa Ta'āla*.
7 The next world.

7. What is veiling you from Him is visibly present in your heart – check and clean.

8. He ﷺ laid out the spiritual journey to Allah. The beginning of the journey to find Him is not confined to a place, nor an act of worship. It all starts in the heart.

9.   What you see is a reflection of you; if your heart is pure, you will see beauty everywhere.

10. What veils seekers from Him is not the lack of
    proofs in His Book, but the lack of seeing the
    illuminations in the proofs. Spiritual blindness is
    in the heart.

11. The heart without love is a tomb. To live beyond this life, love with all your heart. The soul is wise; it is the mind that is arrogant.

12. The Eid celebration is for the one who overcomes the craving to fulfill their lower *nafs* [8] and to satisfy its lowly desires. Celebrations are for the one who collects himself entirely onto Him.

---

8 The lower self.

13. Had He opened for you the serenity and solace
of being with Him, you would have known that
they could not have been found with anyone else.

14. What is preventing you from witnessing His glory are your continuous violations of His instructions, and obsession with His creation.

15. Had you truly known Him, you would not have
disobeyed Him.

16. Those who disobey Him are unaware of the
    consequences; those who avoid obeying Him are
    unaware of His reward.

17. If you have these three things, you have
    succeeded: observing His *hudud* [9], fulfilling His
    u'hud, [10] and witnessing His *shuhūd*. [11]

---

9 Prohibitions.
10 Pledges (plural of *ahd*).
11 To witness the illuminations of His names and
   attributes.

18. Clever is the person who sees things from Allah
Ta'āla first, not from His creation.

19. Whosoever wants to know how his end will likely be: it is mirrored in his present state. Better your present and you will better your end.

20. If you see the creation as the one who is giving and taking from you, then you are veiled. Tear that veil to witness Him.

21. Wise is the one who prioritizes the *huqūq*[12] of Allah over his own desires.

---

12 Rights of Allah.

22. A true believer is busy observing Allah's grace and showing gratitude, rather than seeking self-recognition.

23. If you haven't yet witnessed Him, you are drowning in witnessing the creation.

24. Finding yourself missing Him is a sure sign of *ghafla* [13], for only the absentee misses. Find yourself in His presence.

---

13 Absenteeism, heedlessness.

25. The repentance of the beginner is to move from heedlessness to awareness. That of he who is midway along the path is to move from awareness to presence. That of he who has advanced along the path is to move from presence to absence (i.e. from all but Him).

26. Sufism is not the process of erecting figures
and inaugurating innovated practices into the
religion. Rather, it is to worship Him the way
He wants to be worshipped, and to do it as if you
see Him.

27. You are with the creation if you have not yet witnessed Him. Once you witness Him, the creation will be with you.

28. There is no way you can witness Him while you are witnessing others.

29. His existence in you (i.e., by observing Him) is a pursued dream, yet His existence before and after you is the absolute reality. Rid you of 'you' to get real (Him).

30. The persistent sinner cannot recognize His kindness, generosity, or love.[14] The absentee from His witnessing[15] cannot know Him. The seeker of other than Him will not achieve a lasting or meaningful fulfillment.

---

14 In Arabic: *ihsan*.
15 In Arabic: *muraqaba*.

31. Whoever truly worships Him does not fear
anything; whoever truly loves Him is not
saddened by anything; whoever truly knows
Him does not liken Him to anything; and
whoever believes in Him is safe from everything.

32. It is very easy to be thankful when one is given things, even the most selfish are. A person of love thanks Allah for all the things he was denied.

33. The more love you have, the less veils[16] will exist. It is impossible to love and not receive it. To love Allah, unveils you to see His love.

---

16 In Arabic: *hujub*.

34. The wise one is he who understands his imperfections and faults and strives to improve, leaving no time or energy for identifying them in others.

35. The fool is the one who sees faults and imperfections in others rather than in himself.

36. The fool is the one who sells his *ākhira*[17] for his *dunya*[18]. More foolish is the one who sells his *ākhira* for someone else's *dunya*.

---

17 The next life.
18 This temporary life.

37. Your spiritual state[19] speaks more eloquently than
    your words[20].

---

19 In Arabic: *hāl*.
20 In Arabic: *maqal*.

38. Your lack of preparedness for a real change is depriving you from the real taste.[21]

---

21 Spiritual experience.

39. Whoever has tasted[22] His closeness and love is repulsed by anything that causes distance.

---

22 Spiritually experienced.

40. He did not create us from fire because it is a
    power of destruction; He created us out of clay
    because it has the power for construction.

41. Sufism is an illumination[23] that annihilates you
    before others, then annihilates everything other
    than Him before you, then annihilates you.

---

23 In Arabic: *nūr*.

42. Change your thoughts if you want to experience openings.

43. Love is not a word you say. Love is a *hāl* and a state that collects your body, mind, and soul all together and makes you in conformity with the one you love.

44. The more one focuses on the hysteria of micro-mechanics, the more one diverges away from the core principles of the religion.

45. Your delusions may veil you from Allah. Good thinking, words, and actions along with love tear that veil down.

46. Do not stop shining (illuminating) in and out;
    enlightening the self and others suits you so well.
    You were created to shine – shine on!

47. If you practice the knowledge you know, Allah Ta'āla will give you the knowledge that you do not know. As you amass more information, it will be either for you or against you.

48. If you truly dig deep into your heart, you will
    see the one who sent you love from centuries
    ago, prayed for you, and cared for you before
    you were even born. Do not think that anyone
    could ever be more loving, merciful, caring, and
    protective toward any single one of you than
    Muhammad ﷺ.

49. O my beloved Lord, my Master, my Creator! Maybe You saw me among those whose claims are bigger than their practice, so You abandoned me; or maybe You saw me among those who are ostentatious, so You distanced me; or maybe You saw me relying on other than You, so You tested me; or maybe You saw me among those who are ungrateful for all You given me, so You deprived me (from more of Your limitless generosity); or maybe You saw me among those who are forgetful of, as well as in, Your remembrance (*dhikr*), and are in *ghafla*, so You made me forget even 'me'. O my beloved Lord and Creator, *Sayyidi wa Mawlay*,[24] I have no one to turn to, but You; no one to run to, but You. So, I am running from You to You – please accept me. I have no one who forgives all my sins, but You. Who would forgive all sins and grant redemption

---

24 My Master, the One closest to me.

but You, O Allah – so please forgive me. I want to learn how to love You with all my heart, mind, soul, and with every breath in me, so please guide me and do not leave me to 'me'.

50. There are three 'P's' on the path to Allah: patience, persistence, and perseverance. If you do not have the above, you are not going anywhere, spiritually.

51. The heart is the command. The mind is what points you to do things. The mind points you to the right direction, but can't walk. The heart is the one that walks.

52. The journey to Allah Ta'āla is a journey of the heart. You need to walk to Allah Ta'āla with your heart.

53. How long is the path to Him? Take down the
   veils from your heart, and you're there!

54. Once you purify your heart, the *nūr*[25] of your Lord shines upon it.

---

25 Light/illuminations.

55. When you go to the house of Allah, you are His
    guest. But remember, others are too, so be gentle
    and don't treat anybody harshly. It is the nature
    of the host to be generous and you, too, will find
    Allah most generous. The best thing to take with
    you is your *taqwa*[26] and good companionship.

---

26 Positive contribution to oneself and others.

56. When you come into this world, you enter
crying while others are happy and smiling for
your arrival. Live your life in such a way that,
when you are leaving and others are sad and
crying, you are happy and smiling, because you
are ready to embark on the everlasting life of love
and be with all beloveds, most importantly your
All-Loving creator..

57. Worry about your own heart, not the state of
    other people's hearts, otherwise your heart flips
    from the Creator to creation. Occupying the
    self in remembering the creation is a source of
    disease, in general; mentioning the Creator is a
    source of healing.

58. Allah Ta'āla gave us two ears and one tongue, so that we listen more – twice as much – than we speak. You own your words as long as they are with you. Once you speak, they are recorded and are either for you or against you. Choose them wisely, because it's not worth risking your *ākhira*[27] for a moment of madness.

---

27 The next everlasting life.

59. Don't underestimate even five minutes of
remembrance of Allah Ta'āla with presence — it
could be worth more than your entire life.

60. When we are met with something that is bad, it is not enough to counter it with good. We must counter it with something that is even better than good.

61. Whenever I sin, I am reminded by my weakness and being broken before Him. Let's turn the sin into a win.

62. Live neither in your past, nor in your future; you cannot change the past, nor can you definitively predict the future. If you hold yourself hostage to the sins and bitterness of the past, and occupy yourself with fears of suffering in the future, you will be losing on your presence, hence not living at all. What is worse than suffering itself, is living hostage to such fear. Be assured that Allah Ta'āla is close to you – closer than you think – and closer than you and I could ever comprehend. The question is: are you close to Him?

63. The sign of the knowledgeable one is humbleness;
    the more knowledgeable you are, the more humble
    you are. Were you to look at a husk, if it's filled with
    wheat, it is lowered, if it's empty, it is standing.

Signs on the Path of Love

1. You worry about your present and near future, but *husn al-khatima*[1] is the key milestone that you should concern your heart and mind with achieving.

---

1 Passing on in a good spiritual state.

2. Impurity of the heart and mind is much more detrimental than that of the body, place, or clothes. Real vision is not of the eyes, but of the heart.

3. Successful is not the one who preaches to people and captivates their hearts, but the one who preaches to himself and purifies his heart.

4. Purify your heart from impurities and
    corruption; He will open for you the door to
    unveiling, illumination, and connection.

5. Nothing is more harmful to the hearts than no
    dhikr.[2]

_____

2 The heart being present with the Divine.

6. From a spiritual view, the worlds have multiple
   dimensions: an apparent one and a concealed one.
   Those who look at things through the lens of
   their *nafs*[3] see the apparent, and those who look
   at things through the lens of their heart see more
   – just like the earth whose apparent dimension
   is greenery and water, yet underneath is boiling
   magma.

   _____

   3 Lower desires.

7.   The objective of *dhikr*[4] is to be in His presence with your heart, not solely with your tongue. Is it not the tongue that merely translates the state of the heart?

---

4 Remembrance of The Divine.

8. The best recitation of the Qur'an[5] is that of the heart.

_____

5 The Book revealed to Prophet Muhammad ﷺ, the final Prophet.

9. If you seek perfection, you need to illuminate your heart and mind. If you seek the Prophetic footsteps, you need to illuminate the hearts and minds of others, as well.

10. Real talk is from the heart, not the tongue. Speak from your heart all you want ... I will never be bored.

11. Positive change is a sign of true repentance. If you do not see such transformation, then weep for acceptance.

12. Had He opened for you the door to purification and illumination, you would not go back to impurities. Those who realize what purity is can never go back to filth again.

13. You invoke the blessings of Allah onto His Beloved ﷺ and He showers His blessings onto you, in return. Everyone gives based on their capacity and generosity. Contemplate and appreciate!

14. How much kindness and humility you show before the creation, yet how little before your Creator.

15. He asked you to act in accordance with being a slave to Him, yet you insist on displaying your delusions of master-hood.

16. Live your life with Allah Ta'āla; follow His instructions and be noble with His creation.

17. There is no way to collect yourself entirely onto Allah, without observing Him and what He asked of you.

18. Whoever is transparent with Allah will be
    sufficed from all worries.

19. Humiliated, indeed, is the one who relies on the creation. Think good of the creation, but rely only on Him.

20. If you insist on evil deeds, just adding good ones to them will not help you much in your spiritual travel to Him, for entry into His presence requires purity.

21. What helps you on the spiritual journey to Allah is the quality of your deeds, not just the quantity.

22. Prioritizing the authentic Sunnah[6] and perfecting its application is the point. Allah said[7] 'best in deeds', not 'more deeds'.

قال الله تعالى: لِيَبْلُوَكُمْ أَيُّكُمْ أَحْسَنُ عَمَلًا

Allah says, which may mean: "[…] so that He may put you to test, to see who does better deeds […]".[8]

---

6 The Prophetic Path.
7 In meaning.
8 A portion of surah al-Mulk, verse 2 [in meaning].

23. You cannot spiritually journey to Allah if you have not yet practiced and mastered the station of sincere repentance.

24. The first prerequisite for those who wish to go on the path of illumination to Allah is prayer, even if only two units, at the end of the night.

25. Do not ever plan a sin.

26. If you are with Him, you will not need anyone
    else but Him; but if you don't find Him, then
    even if you have the whole world, you have
    nothing. Find Him.

27. Our source of light and motivation is the ever-lasting Book of Allah Ta'āla.

28. Whoever loves Him does not intend to disobey Him. If he sins, he sincerely repents. When he sincerely repents, Allah forgives.

29. Among the best things that Allah loves from His worshipper is to trust Him and rely on Him.

30. Love is the language of the souls, as well as all that is within the universe; the limitations of language do not apply.

31.   Love is felt, but may not be seen; it is lived, but
      is never routine.

32. The only way to prevail over your *nafs*[9] and discipline it is to possess love in the heart. Love, not just information, will make you overcome any spiritual challenge.

---

9 Self.

33. Only amassing information generates arrogance
    and pride, whereas love that is nestled in the
    heart generates humility and awareness of others.
    Information may lead to wars, but love leads to
    peace.

34. Gnosis[10] is based on love and is the affair of the soul.

قال الله تعالى: وَيَسْأَلُونَكَ عَنِ الرُّوحِ ٭ قُلِ الرُّوحُ مِنْ أَمْرِ رَبِّي

Allah says, which may mean: "and they ask you about the soul.[...] Say the soul is the affair of my Lord [...]".[11]

---

10 In Arabic: *ma'rifa*.

11 A portion of surah al-Isra, verse 85 [in meaning].

35. Peace, both inner and outer, is not just the absence of violence, but the presence and experience of love. Peace begins with love, and love begins with peace.

36. The non-verbal talk between lovers is the real talk – souls talk. No words can ever describe an experienced reality of love. Practice…

37. I profess the religion of love wherever it takes me along the way; that is my belief and my path above, and the faith I practice every day.

38. Prayer[12] and love both require purity[13]
     beforehand, otherwise they are invalid.

---

12 In Arabic: *salat*.
13 In Arabic: *tahara*.

39. The decimated and spiritually bankrupt are those
    who are consumed in their sins by fulfilling
    instant gratifications.

40. Sincere repentance always brings a victory;
    ignoring to do so is always a loss.

41. The most lethal spiritual impediments are the sins
that one belittles.

42. A Muslim is the one who is transparent with others in private without revealing their imperfections in public.

43. The real loss is not when you lose some *dunya*[14] for the sake of the *akhira*,[15] as there could always be an opportunity for make-up in this life. But when you forfeit the *akhira* by being consumed in the *dunya*, then there is no make-up.

---

14 This temporary life.
15 The everlasting life.

44. The ugliest *dunya* is seeking it with all one's got, while pretending detachment from it.

45. The guide to Him is not the one who has the words and looks, but the one who continuously struggles to prioritize the Qur'an and the Sunnah.

46. Continuous repentance brings uninterrupted sustenance.

47. Foolish is the one who is intoxicated by the glory of the *dunya* [16] coming to him; and worse yet is the one who is sad for missing it.

---

16 This temporary life.

48. Sincere preparedness will lead to continuous sustenance.

49. The most foul-smelling of all is a claim with no
     reality.

50. Who does not discipline his *nafs*, it will discipline him. And who does not demand from it, it will demand from him.

51. He knew your weakness so He decreased the number of prayers to five, and knew your needs, so increased their reward to fifty and beyond.

52. Let the fruits of your actions speak louder than your statements about doing good actions.

53. It is never what's in the world that is the problem — it is the attachment to it. *Tahalli* [17] comes after *takhalli* [18].

---

17 Beautification.
18 Purification.

54. Giving is living – the more you give, the more you live. Learn from the Prophets and those who walked in their steps, like Imam al-Husayn.

55. This *dīn* is not about mere association, but about positive contribution.[19]

---

19 Faith.

56. Beautiful things are beautiful as they are without any additions. Beauty is in simplicity.

57. Islam is a religion that came to give life, not take it away.

58. It is never about, *fatwa* [20] but about *taqwa*.[21]

---

20 Legal judgement of scholars.
21 God-concientousness positive contribution.

59. Any interpretation of the Book[22] or of the
    Sunnah that is void of compassion is illegitimate.

---

22 Referring to the Qur'an.

60. Do not treat others based on your perceptions or
the perceptions of others; treat people the way
Allah would be pleased with you treating people.

61. Not once did Allah say in the Qur'an: He 'hates'.

62. Go to your beloved – there is no beloved other than Him! There is no one who loves you, cares for you, and knows about you more than Him. There is no one who longs for your closeness to Him, more than Him.

63. Your path to perfection is in following the steps of Adam, *alayhi salām*. When he made a mistake, he repented.

64. We do not follow each other, but we share knowledge with each other.

65. Do not follow me, for I am a sinner; but share knowledge, love, and compassion with me, and we all win.

66. Religion is the art of the noblest possible, the most virtuous possibly attainable – the art of the next righteous best. Therefore, religion does not necessarily mean 'the religious'.

67. In every heart there is a light of love. Rekindle
one at a time, rekindle on ...

68. Love is an amazingly mysterious thing. It rules and is not ruled, visits frequently but does not stay, touches but does not hold, starts but does not end.

69. Love sharpens the senses and sensations, but hurts the heart. It is beyond words, therefore, it is indescribable with them.

70. Love is the language of the souls of the universe, hence tongues can never articulate it.

71. The path of love is a labour of the heart, not
    of the mind. Amassing more *'ilm*,[23] although
    needed, does not necessarily make you a lover
    of Him. The path to Allah is a labor of the heart
    primarily, not of the body or mind as much.
    "Allah does not look at your body, but [your]
    hearts."[24]

---

23 Knowledge.
24 Hadīth found in Sahih Muslim.

72. Hate does not extinguish hate. Darkness
    does not extinguish darkness. Prejudice does
    not extinguish prejudice. Negativity does
    not extinguish negativity. It's only love that
    extinguishes hate. It's only light that extinguishes
    darkness. It's only knowledge that extinguishes
    ignorance.

73. This *dīn* of ours is a *dīn*[25] of love – no love, no *dīn*.
The Beloved sent His Beloved ﷺ out of love, to
teach love, with love, for the sake of love.

----

25 Faith.

74. A sign of loving sayyidana Rasūl'Allah ﷺ is prioritizing his ways. In these times of mass confusion, the Book and the authentic Sunnah are safe and saving.

75. The *dunya*[26] is a place of sacrifice, difficulty, pain, giving, and love… and love of Allah makes it bearable.

---

26 This temporary life.

76. It is bewildering how much I long for them and ask yearningly about them, while they're still with me; my eye tears for them, while they are its light; my heart aches from their distance, while they are within my rib cage. If they demand the rights of being their lover, I will say, "I am but a *faqir* [27] who doesn't have anything." If they leave me in the prison of their distance, I'll ask them by their beloved. [28]

---

27 A person in need.
28 By an unknown poet.

77. The one truly pursuing the *ākhira* [29] does not
    have time for animosity, grudges, or hate, but
    forgives, moves on, and loves.

_____

29 The everlasting life of love.

78. There is one path to the Beloved Ta'āla: the path of love. Travelling the path of love has a pre-requisite: light travel. Selflessness, or love for all and malice towards none, is key. Only when love transcends all limits does it reach truth. The beloved Messenger ﷺ is the Messenger of love, the Qur'an is a book of love, the universe is playing the melody of love, and the whole test is a test of love. The heart that is void of true love, is void of true life.

79. How can I forget a love that is my heart and
    soul? How can I forget while He is reminding me
    of Him in every beauty and everything beautiful?

80. Love is the most powerful energy that Allah created. Love rids us of all pain, removes all weights, brightens our life, and turns all dis-ease into ease.

81. Love is a moral law. It connects you to the
soul of the universe, gives wings to the heart,
unlimited skies to the mind, and life to life itself.

82. Live your love and you will love to live; with love there is only life.

83. Sufism: when you find Him, love Him, and live and pass on with Him. Once you find Him there is no death, so live forever with love.

84. I thought of You so much that I have become all consumed in Your love. Little by little, You arrived and, for a second, I looked for me, but there is only You.

85. Angels could not praise You enough, who am I?
Prophets admitted incapacity to thank You
enough, who am I? I am faults and claims. You
are love and forgiveness.

86. Dedicate a part of your home to being a *masjid*;[30] that's where you shed tears and write letters of love to Allah.

---

30 A home of prayers.

Illuminations

1. The heart is a tree that is irrigated by the water of worship and good deeds; its fruits are the emergence of vivid spiritual states.

2. The beginners on this journey of love are concerned with correcting the state of their deeds, and the more advanced are concerned with correcting the state of their hearts.

3. There are four cardiotoxic things: excessive food, excessive talk, excessive sleep, and excessive mingling with others. Their treatment is also four: talk to Him not just to His creation, meditate through silence of the tongue and *dhikr*[1] of the heart, decrease your food intake, and take a vacation with Him and spend it only talking to, seeing, and being with Him.

---

1 Remembrance.

4. Those who are awake may attain *shuhūd*.[2] But, for
   those who aren't, how can they witness in their
   hearts when their ears are asleep?

_____

2 Witnessing.

5. If you want to heal your heart then travel to the
land of repentance, live in the state of presence,
and wear the garments of neediness and humility.

6. *Iman*[3] and the heart have a paradoxical relationship: for one to be firm, the other will have to be soft. There is no other way.

---

3 Faith.

7. If you want to explore the universe and beyond, open a path from your heart to your soul, then fly! Love is faster than light and stronger than gravity.

8. Silence of the tongue is a minimum condition to be in the Muhammadan Presence ("O you who have attained to faith! Do not raise your voices above the voice of the Prophet, and neither speak loudly to him, as you would speak loudly to one another, lest all your [good] deeds come to nought without your perceiving it.") [4] Silence of the heart is a minimum condition to be in Allah's Presence ("Allah – there is no deity save Him; to Him belong the most beautiful names!") [5]

قال الله تعالى: يَا أَيُّهَا الَّذِينَ آمَنُوا لَا تَرْفَعُوا أَصْوَاتَكُمْ

فَوْقَ صَوْتِ النَّبِيِّ وَلَا تَجْهَرُوا لَهُ بِالْقَوْلِ كَجَهْرِ

بَعْضِكُمْ لِبَعْضٍ أَنْ تَحْبَطَ أَعْمَالُكُمْ وَأَنْتُمْ لَا تَشْعُرُونَ

و قال الله تعالى: اللَّهُ لَا إِلَهَ إِلَّا هُوَ ۞ لَهُ الْأَسْمَاءُ الْحُسْنَىٰ

---

4 Surah al-Hujarat, verse 2 [in meaning].
5 Surah TaHa, verse 8 [in meaning].

9. Disobedience that generates shamefacedness
    before Allah, as well as humility and self-
    awareness of one's ignorance, may be better than
    obedience that causes arrogance (Ibn 'Ata).

10. Had you witnessed some of the meanings of Godhood, then the great worlds and all that is in them, on them, and between them, would look differently, immediately. This is a taste of *Allahu Akbar*.[6]

---

6 God is greater (than everything).

11. Your birthday is not the day you were physically born, but the day you started loving Him.

12. Had He opened for you the door of being
present with Him, you would be marvelled with
His surprises and wonders.

13. If you want to be given by Him, live needy of Him and if you seek victory from Him, have humility before Him.

14. Don't expect days of *ghafla*[7] to yield nights of *dhikr*[8]. Plant your seeds during the day; you will collect your gifts at night.

---

7 Heedlessness and absenteeism from Him.
8 The heart being present with the Divine.

15. When you remember Him, it is because He
    opened for you that door and allowed you to
    enter into the court of His Presence. When
    you're not in remembrance, you've been deprived
    of entry – check your credentials.

16. The gnostic[9] has no *dunya*[10] and no *ākhira*[11] because his *dunya* is used for his *ākhira*, and his *ākhira* is used for closeness to Him.

---

9 A friend of Allah Taʿāla.
10 This temporary life.
11 The next life.

17. The five prayers are the time and place of
    munajāt[12]. Their spiritual dimensions can be
    narrow or almost limitless, average or overflowing
    with illuminations, true realizations, and wisdom.
    You and your Lord.

---

12 Talking to Allah.

18. The foundation of the spiritual journey to Him is
    rooted in *dhikr*.[13] *Dhikr* leads to *ma'rifa*;[14] *ma'rifa*
    leads to *shukr*.[15]

---

13 The heart being present with the Divine.
14 Gnosis.
15 Gratitude.

19. He diversified the manifestations of His
    magnificence in His creation in order to lead you
    to the absolute uniqueness of His oneness.

20. I want You, O Allah, the way You want me to want You.

21. Not every *murīd* [16] is *murad*, [17] but every *murad*
    is *murīd*; the permitted is not the one who seeks
    ijaza, [18] but the one sought by it.

---

16 Seeker.
17 Chosen.
18 Permission.

22. Fear is a prodding whip; hope is a singing cameleer; and love is a driving force.

23. A certain degree of darkness is maybe needed to see the stars. Stars shine with a light of guidance. Make sure you are looking, comparing, and reflecting.

24. The Muhammadan Presence is where you acquire *adāb*.[19] The *Rabbani*[20] presence is where you listen to the *khitāb*.[21]

---

19 Etiquette.
20 Lordly.
21 Speech.

25. The *awliyā'*[22] of Allah do not stand between you and Allah Ta'āla; they stand behind you to push you towards Allah Ta'āla.

---

22 Saints or friends of Allah Ta'āla.

26. If your love and attachment to a creation is severed, do not be sad. Maybe He is opening for you to love and be attached to Him instead.

27. Whoever truly struggles to show Him his true love of Him will be offered drink from His generosity and breezes of His closeness and love.

28. True love is when you treasure private time with your Beloved. No true lover shares these moments with anyone. Treading the path of love does not necessarily correlate to talking the talk. Those who really walk don't have much time to talk.

29. Love refines you, but also causes heartache.

30. Love is beyond words, therefore all of them put
    together cannot describe it.

31. I said to my Beloved: "O my Love, my heart
     needs Your love or it will die, but what good am
     I then? Unless that pleases You."

32. You behave based on your conception of, as well as your relationship with, Him. If you think of Him as the Loving and the Compassionate, then so are you.[23]

---

23 The attributes of Allah are not similar to the creation.

33. Faith devoid of love equals no faith at all.

34. A loving heart is the beginning of all knowledge.

35. The key to all is inhaling love and exhaling gratitude.

36. The reality of worship is seeking His love. And the reality of dealing with people is love.

37. The less love flowing through you, the less
    knowledge you have.

38. The well of love has no pulley or bucket; the only way to drink is to throw yourself into it.

39. Sufis believe in, dream about, teach, preach,
    breathe, live, and all they talk is about is, love.
    This reality is better than the sweetest dreams.

40. If the outer manifestation is purely Muhammadi,
the inner is entirely *Rabbani*. The color – in and
out – is love. Its place: the unity of the cosmos.

41. Had He honoured you by allowing you to be
    close to Him, He would not dishonour you by
    throwing you to others.

42. Don't believe that people missed out on success, whether in the *dīn*[24] or the *dunya*,[25] rather, they missed the *tawfiq*[26] of Allah Ta'āla.

---

24 Religious/spiritual matters.

25 Worldly matters.

26 Facilitation or opportunity.

43. The reason you find some of the accounts of the
    Prophets and *awliyā'* as strange is because you are
    in a different world, living a different life. You
    are looking for them in your world, but cannot
    find them, and they are looking for you in their
    world, but cannot find you. Had you been
    accompanying them in their travels through the
    dunya, you wouldn't have needed to hear about
    their miracles. Had you shared with them the
    pain, you would have shared with them the gain.

44. If Allah's special care is with you, then minimum deeds suffice. If not, then a lot of deeds won't help.

45. *Rahma* [27] is the prerequisite for *'ilm*. [28]

قال الله تعالى: الرَّحْمَنُ ٭ عَلَّمَ الْقُرْآنَ

Allah says, which may mean:
"The Lovingly Compassionate. It is He Who has
taught the Qur'an." [29]

---

27 Loving compassion.
28 Knowledge.
29 Surah al-Rahman, verse 1-2 [in meaning].

46. The Sunnah is not to face the sinner with the might of righteousness, but with the beauty and mercy of forgiveness.

47. Many people are perplexed about religion. The essential part of religion is about learning to give out love and learning to let it come in.

48. The greatest enemy we have is ignorance, then
    arrogance, and thirdly: ignorance.

49. The point is not to be kind and generous when someone agrees with you, but to pay attention to the One who is kind and generous, even when you disobey Him.

50. Good deeds and spirituality are just like
     knowledge and *adab*[30] – they never separate until
     death does them apart.

_____

30 Refinement/etiquette.

51. Your *nūr*[31] in the world of physics is directly dependent on the strength of your *nisbah*[32] in the world of souls.

---

31 Light.
32 Grounding/link.

52. *Safā'*[33] and *wafā'*[34] are inseparable partners. *Safā'*
tells *wafā'*: "do not grieve, indeed Allah is with us".

قَالَ اللهُ تَعَالَى: ثَانِيَ اثْنَيْنِ إِذْ هُمَا فِي الْغَارِ إِذْ يَقُولُ لِصَاحِبِهِ
لَا تَحْزَنْ إِنَّ اللَّهَ مَعَنَا ٭ فَأَنْزَلَ اللَّهُ سَكِينَتَهُ عَلَيْهِ وَأَيَّدَهُ
بِجُنُودٍ لَمْ تَرَوْهَا وَجَعَلَ كَلِمَةَ الَّذِينَ كَفَرُوا السُّفْلَىٰ ٭

Allah says, which may mean: "[…] they two were in
the cave and he said to his companion 'have no fear for
Allah is with us': then Allah sent down His peace upon
him and strengthened him with forces which ye saw
not and humbled to the depths the word of
the unbelievers. [...]".[35]

---

33 Purity.

34 Loyalty.

35 A portion of surah al-Tawba, verse 40 [in meaning].

53. For every guiding star that is illuminating the skies, there is a satanic whisper on earth. Look to the sky for light.

قال الله تعالى: وَلِتَصْغَىٰ إِلَيْهِ أَفْئِدَةُ الَّذِينَ لَا يُؤْمِنُونَ بِالْآخِرَةِ وَلِيَرْضَوْهُ وَلِيَقْتَرِفُوا مَا هُمْ مُقْتَرِفُونَ

Allah says, which may mean: "That the hearts of those who believe not in the Hereafter may incline thereto, and that they may take pleasure therein, and that they may earn what they are earning."[36]

---

36 Surah al-An'am, verse 113 [in meaning].

54. With Allah, the impossible becomes possible;
    without Him, nothing is possible.

55. *Ahlul dunya* [37] may not conquer the *dunya* after all; *ahlul ākhirah* [38] may fail to secure the heavens; *ahl Allah* [39] see the *dunya* and the *akhira* at their feet.

---

37 People of the world.
38 People of the hereafter.
39 People of Allah.

56. The ocean symbolizes the next life; its end cannot be seen and what its depth has is unknown.

57. The voice of truth irritates the sleep of tyrants.

58. The *kalima* of *shahada* [40] is an intellectual and spiritual state, not just an utterance.

---

40 Testimony of faith.

59. Those who try to go to the depths of knowledge
   ought to be looking for the secrets in the stores
   of *rahma*.[41]

---

41 Unconditional compassion.

60. The wealthy [person] is not the one who has the most, but the one who needs the least.

61. Life is a journey that begins with love, which carries us through all barriers, shines through all darkness, and jumps all hurdles to arrive at its destination.

62. His ﷻ *rahma* [42] is not just waiting for you in the *dunya*,[43] it is also waiting for you at the beginning of the *hisāb*.[44]

---

42 Loving mercy.
43 This temporary life.
44 Reckoning.

63. The light of Rasul Allah ﷺ never fades. This is why he is your road to *Jannah*.[45]

---

45 Heaven.

64. *Munajāt*: "I wish to really know You truly in my life, then I can die". *Ilham*: [46] "those who know Me do not die".

---

46 A meaning put in the heart.

65. Love is the prayer of the heart that is totally and entirely pure.

66. The Prophet ﷺ remained the same throughout
    his life. He ﷺ did not allow the world to change
    him. Power and money did not change him;
    hardship and loss did not change him; he came
    into the *dunya* [47] pure, and he left the *dunya* pure.

---

47 This temporary life.

67. *Haqq*[48] does not need sponsorship from *batil*.[49] When people fight and slander then it has nothing to do with Allah – it has to do with the *dunya*.

---

48 Truth.
49 Evil.

68. Your soul and my soul are very, very old friends. After all, we all come from the same Nafs.

69. Stop talking about Allah to His creation, and start talking to Allah, the Creator.

70. He ﷺ is never disconnected from those of his
    Ummah [50] who love him.

---

50 His nation.

71. Our Sufi masters taught us that love is the key
    ingredient to life. All good things stem from
    love, and all evil things stem from no love.

72. The Most Loving prohibited "frowning and turning away"[51] in the face of a blind man. What about the seeing? Smile, it's Sunnah.

---

51 Surah 'Abasa, verse 1 [in meaning].

73. Allah is not matter, Allah does matter; Allah is not energy, Allah gives energy, energy.

74. Which music is definitively *harām*?[52] The one made by the noise of spoons hitting the empty plates of the starving and every voice of *batil*.[53]

---

52 Forbidden.
53 Evil/corruption.

75. A mix of *jalāl* [54] and *jamāl* , [55] leads to *kamāl*. [56]
    Welcome to the Prophetic presence.

---

54 Majesty.
55 Beauty.
56 Perfection.

76. Abu Bakr came to meet the Prophet ﷺ simply
to behold his ﷺ blessed face. Your shaykh is not
just the teacher you only heard knowledge from,
but the one you imbibed from. Your shaykh is
not the one whose words are in your ears and
on your tongue, but the one who lives deep
in you, with his vision, thoughts, and breath.
Your shaykh is not the one who invited you to
join him, but the one who removed all veils,
distances, and protocols between you and him.
Your shaykh is not the one whose speech affects
you, but whose *himma* [57] raises you. Your shaykh
is the one who continuously keeps cleansing and
cleaning the mirror of your heart, until your
vision of the truth becomes clearer and clearer,
and until the *Rabbani* illuminations shine all over
your heart and overwhelms it. Your shaykh is the
one who taught you about Allah Ta'ala and His
People, so you followed their way, and walked
with you until you become close to Allah Ta'ala

---

57 Perseverance, persistence, vision, and motivations.

– very close – and then threw you in the oceans of the lights and illuminations of the magnificent Presence of Allah Ta'āla, telling you, "Here you are, and your Lord."[58]

---

58 Paraphrased from Ibn Ata'.

77. The *'ulema* [59] of the *salihīn* [60] do not stand between the Creator and the creation, but they stand behind the creation and push the creation to the Creator.

---

59 Scholars.
60 Pious people.

78. Love whoever you want to love, but do not
    interject a new standard into the *Ummah*. The
    standard is the Qur'an and the authentic Sunnah.

79. Islam wants us to see the good in everyone, in all humanity, both Muslims and non-Muslims, as if they are either *awliyā' Allah*[61] or potential *awliyā' Allah*.

---

61 Saints, friends of, or close to Allah.

Live Your Love

1. Love purifies and perfects. It is behind the perfection found in all things throughout the universe.

2. The Qur'an: a book of love dedicated to you, with love. – Your Loving Creator

3. He ﷻ created you by love, with love, to love, for love.

4. Life is meant to be a journey and an experience of love, followed by a never-ending story of love.

5. Love is a supergravity that attracts, pulls, permeates, and bundles the whole universe. You are part of it, tap in.

6. Words can never describe love; logic can never
    encompass love; imagination can never limit love.
    All I know is that it exists.

7. Is love the supreme form of energy? I don't
    know. But I know it is more real than the
    sun, the moon, and gravity. It is more like the
    wind, the breeze, the waves, and light. It nears
    the distant, heals the heart, and heartens the
    destitute.

8. The universe started with love, was built with love, and our very existence only continues with love. Take away love from anything and watch it collapse.

9. In this vast universe, there is a limitless dimension filled with love where souls very close to each other are attracted together.

10. Give and you will receive. You are not more generous than the One who gave you everything. Withhold and you will be withheld from. It's your choice, so don't blame the Heavens for it.

11. First morning thought: Allah Ta'āla is really good to me. Thank You O Allah.

12. Talk a lot about what you love, not about what you don't. The more you talk about your love, the higher you rise; the more you talk about what you don't love, the more you plummet. You are a companion of and a hostage to what you say or think.

13. Love is the fulfillment of the eternal covenant.

14. Love is not a sign of weakness, but a manifestation of strength. It is the light of life that guides you to all good, the force in life that leads you to all success, and the drive pushing you to all positivity.

15. Every perfection you want to be, say, do, or have stems from love, and if it is to last, it needs to be for love.

16. Love is like a massive gravitational field. Once you're in its path, love from all directions and ways will come to you.

17. Things around you (people, signs, objects, colors, sounds, etc.) don't just happen. In general, they are responding to you. Your thoughts, words, and actions sketch your life-path.

18. Our daily life is full of choices between love and
no love. The more you choose love, the more
you inwardly harness light and energy, until you
become completely *nūr–ala–nūr.*[1]

---

1 Light upon light.

19. You don't have to take everything life sends your way by reciprocating negativity for negativity. Just pick love and all roads that lead to love, and never look back.

20. People think and talk about what they love. If what they love is good and lasting, so they will be, too. If not, they're wasting their life.

21. If you think and talk about what you love, it will come to you. As for the levels of love, the sky is not the limit, it's just the beginning.

22. There is no power [2] greater than faith, and there is no faith greater than love.

---

2 Created power.

23. Fix your relationship with Allah Ta'āla by starting to have *husn al-dhann*[3] of Him. Your good thinking of Him is based on His kindness and generosity, not yours. You are given not according to your good deeds, but more so according to how much you love. Feel the love.

---

3 Good thinking.

24. Your *husn al-dhann* of Allah Ta'āla ought to be the good feeling that always lives in you – it's your fuel. Live it, don't abuse it.

25. How dare you quantify something that the Heavens didn't quantify! How much should I love Allah?! How much should I love His Rasul ﷺ?! If you measure love, then how little you love.

26. Use love and the energy it provides to change your condition to the best of conditions.

27. If you, or the people around you, surround you with negativity, save yourself by fortifying love in you. Love for Allah Ta'āla and love for His beloveds. Start by thinking of them, then grow your love for them. You cannot replace every negative, just increase love or add more love connections and watch all negatives go away.

28. Since love is an energy found in all creation, everything you truly love loves you and wants you just as much, if not more.

29. The real struggle on the path of love to Allah
    Ta'āla is not making difficult changes in your life,
    as much as it is allowing love to shine through
    you and through all you think, say, and do.

30. Once you experience Allah's love and the love of His Beloved in a special way, then welcome to Paradise – the happiest place on Earth. The next step: give and you'll receive – this is His promise.

31. A change in your thinking[4] of Allah Ta'āla is a
change in your destiny.

---

4 In Arabic: *husn al-dhann.*

32. If you want to discover the universe and many of its secrets, then enter the dimension of love.

33. It's never about what is thought of, said about, or done to you. What comes out of you in thoughts, words, and actions determines your path in this life and the hereafter. Dispositions matter more than circumstances.

34. Don't waste your present in regret about the past. Repent, and you are forgiven. Live the time you have, not the delusion of the one you don't.

35. Blame, destructive criticism, grudges, finding faults, and complaining are all forms of negativity that will only increasingly bring you down, waste your precious time, and attract more trouble to you – it's companionship after all.

36. Most people whose feelings are based on what happens to them or around them have a severed relationship with Allah Ta'āla. Not only do they reinforce and renew their strife by harboring negative feelings, but they neglect Allah's call for them to change themselves so that their surroundings change.

37. The Qur'an informs us that thoughts and
    words have powerful effects on you and your
    surroundings. If you want to change things
    around you, throw all negative thoughts and
    words out of your mind and mouth, forever.
    Free yourself of evil.

38. *Husn al-dhann* [5] is not just of Allah Ta'āla, but the
    Prophet ﷺ asked us to have good thinking of all.
    This is essential for changing our condition.

---

5 Good thinking.

39. Allah Ta'āla is the Creator of everything, and His bounties are endless. Be transparent with Him; ask Him for anything good your heart desires and watch it come to you, and more. Potentialities and possibilities are limitless. If it's good and you can think of it, you can have it.

40. True belief in the unseen turns it into seen.
    Welcome to faith.

41. If you want to receive love or what you love, you must fill yourself up with so much love that it overspills onto others consciously and unconsciously.

42. *Ahl al-mahabbah*[6] surround themselves with things, people, and relevant objects that remind them of what they love, so they see, feel, smell, and hear their love. Live your love. The opposite is also true.

---

6 The people of love.

43. Once you have completed *du'a*[7] properly, you have moved into a new world that contains what you have asked for. Even if you can't see it yet, know you will receive it, and thank Him plenty for already granting it to you.

---

7 Asking process.

44. The delay in receiving is due to your delay in trust and faith in Him.

45. *Du'a* is a feeling because it is a matter of the heart in the first place. If your feeling (heart) is good, then your whole body and world is good, just like the Prophet ﷺ said.

46. Doubts are like highway robbers – they steal all
    the good you've accumulated.

47. Love manifested by feeling and expressed by thoughts, words, and actions has a cumulative effect. The more you add, the closer you are to light.

48. Your daily *wird*[8] is your absolute key of
    meditation for a few minutes every day. Imbibe
    love, foster love, and grow love until you
    feel the breeze of love. Don't turn it into lip
    service, otherwise you will not only lose out on
    connecting to love, but also on receiving all that
    comes with it.

---

8 Routine litany.

49. There is a simple way to rid yourself of negative thoughts: ignore permanently and throw the remains in the garbage.

50. Once you enter the dimension of love, the illusion of place and time will be exposed. The distinction between here and there, or between past, present, and future, will reveal itself as never existent.

51. There are many illusions in the world around us that we take for real, including the world itself, hence our suffering increases. The only true reality is Allah, and to Him we all shall return.

52. The more you turn your back on love, the more you linger in suffering and go against your promised, happy destiny.

53. Fault finders are love-deficient.

54. Repentance is absolution from sins, it is therefore very negative and dangerous to one's faith to doubt His generosity, forgiveness, kindness, and love.

55. Your secret rests in your heart. Polish your screens and watch the light emanate to and from the universe. No one can take that from you; your soul power is all yours. You and Allah... enjoy!

56. After all the years of hard work, guidance, sacrifices,
    suffering, and light that the Prophet ﷺ made for us
    all, he never said, 'You owe me.'
    This is love for you.

57. Allah Ta'āla promised to answer every genuine
prayer. Never, ever doubt Him, but go ahead
confidently knowing that His *rahmah*[9] will
overwhelm you again, and again.

---

9 His unconditional Compassion and loving mercy.

58. Love beautifies. The most imperfect surpasses
perfection with love.

59. The path of love is a path of happiness. Turn away from it, and you're turning your back on happiness in both abodes.

60. To live your love is not just to say, "I love", but to truly love like you've never loved before.

61. The mind sometimes acts as a veil from the lights
    the soul emanates onto you. A healthy mind is
    one where love is shining everywhere in it.

62. The key to genuine love is absolute gratitude. It
is no coincidence that 'The Opening'[10] (al-Fatiha)
starts with, *'al-hamd '*.[11] For this reason, if this
is the only surah you read (i.e., experience) in
your prayers, it is enough, as this is all the prayers
you will ever need. Yet Allah Ta'ala informed us
in the Qur'an that abundant gratitude calls for
abundant giving.

---

10 The first chapter in the Qur'an, which is called
al-Fatiha in Arabic.
11 Absolute gratitude.

63. Realizing that your life – as it is today – is a result
of the labor of others, both living and dead, and
that your life and theirs, inner and outer, is a
continuously coming gift of His, ought to lead
you to gratefulness toward others and absolute
gratitude to Him.

64. Manifesting gratefulness shouldn't be limited to when you receive what you want. Gratitude means to be absolutely grateful for absolutely everything you have received, are receiving, and will receive.

65. Only those whose gratitude is abundant realize the abundance of what they receive. A life with gratitude is a rich life.

66. If you want to learn about love, then observe the purity and innocence of young children.

67. Vehicles may take you from one place to another, but love will take you everywhere.

68. If you fully believe in Him and fully trust in Him, nothing possible is out of reach.

69. If you can turn your day into a love experience, you have won. Look around you every day and take note of all the things you love, and give back. Every minute, every person, and every situation is an opportunity to practice and accumulate. Love with all your heart.

74. Those who withhold love and kindness from others, withhold love and kindness from themselves. Those who think, say, and do evil to others, only truly hurt themselves.

75. Don't let your reactions and emotions abuse you.
Use them to enjoy your life, not ruin it.

76. Use the eternal divine love, the ancient Muhammadan love, and *du'a*[12] as your shield to navigate through the negativity in this temporary life. Remember that a negative cannot neutralize a negative.

---

12 Prayers.

77. The loving Prophet's ﷺ wish was for a better world, where all the creation loves one another.

78. Your stress, distress, and anxiety are largely due
    to a diminished reliance on, and faith in Him due
    to not seeing His enveloping love and care. Open
    the eye of your heart to this and watch all the
    stress disappear.

79. You see the creation with the eyes of your head,[13]
    and you see the Creator with the eyes of your
    heart.[14] Use both sights, but realize which one
    relays only the truth.

---

13 In Arabic: *basar.*
14 In Arabic: *basira.*

80. Many physicists say the human being is a micro-cosm of the universe. Many Sufis say the exact opposite.

81. Don't look for miracles, but look for love, for where you find true love, miracles are a common, daily thing.

82. As love grows in you, illumination ensues, and the delusional distinction between life and death disappears. The question was never whether we will transition and live on but, rather, will you enjoy it?

83. The real elixir of life, fountain of youth, water
of longevity, light of happiness, and illumination
of the heart and soul, is the overflowing love
within you that gushes forth for all. This is
alchemy at its finest.

84. If there is negativity and positivity in you, do not adopt negativity by letting it fester, grow, and have attention.

85. Instead, adopt the positivity in you and grow
    it to counter and overcome the opposing
    negativity. You shouldn't try to fight the divine
    decree, but should flow with it looking for love.
    It's abundantly present, just open the eye of your
    heart to see.

86. There are people who turn simplicity into complexity, harmony into dissonance, love into aversion, and opportunity into impossibility. Your mission is exactly the opposite.

87. In the Qur'an, Allah Ta'āla never spoke about Himself in terms of love versus hate. It's always love or no love. Love is good, and everything else is just not love, for there is only one thing you should pay attention to and one thing that matters: love.